The MAILBOX®

The Education Center®

Every
Seasonal & Holiday

Timesaving tools for year-round skills practice

- "Listen and Do" pages
- Beginning sound practice
- Letter recognition practice
- Picture cards to sort and sequence
- Fold-and-go booklets
- Quick crafts

- Fine-motor fun
- Class booklet pages
- Math mats and cards

Plus extra ways to use the teaching tools!

Managing Editor: Kelly Robertson

Editorial Team: Becky S. Andrews, Diane Badden, Kimberley Bruck, Karen A. Brudnak, Kitty Campbell, Pam Crane, Lynette Dickerson, Sarah Foreman, Theresa Lewis Goode, Ada Goren, Tazmen Hansen, Marsha Heim, Lori Z. Henry, Debra Liverman, Dorothy C. McKinney, Thad H. McLaurin, Brenda Miner, Sharon Murphy, Jennifer Nunn, Mark Rainey, Greg D. Rieves, Hope Rodgers, Eliseo De Jesus Santos II, Rebecca Saunders, Barry Slate, Donna K. Teal, Joshua Thomas, Zane Williard

www.themailbox.com

©2009 The Mailbox® Books
All rights reserved.
ISBN10 #1-56234-879-5 • ISBN13 #978-156234-879-3

Manufactured in the United States
10 9 8 7 6 5 4 3 2 1

What's

fun practice pages

Activities for every season and 19 holidays!

class booklet pages

Inside

more ways to use the tools

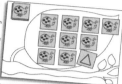

Bonus Activities
Finish the Picture

math mats and cards

quick crafts

cards to sort and sequence

Flowers For Mom

Materials: 9" x 12" sheet of construction paper folded in half (card),
colorful tissue paper squares, markers, scissors, glue

Directions: Decorate the vase as desired; then cut it out and glue it
near the bottom of the front of the card. Draw green stems
and leaves above the vase. Crumple tissue paper squares
to make flowers and glue one to the top of each stem.
When the glue is dry, illustrate and personalize the inside of
the card.

Table of Contents

What's Inside 2

Fall 5
Bonus activities 19

Grandparents Day 21

Halloween 25

Thanksgiving 31
Bonus activities 42

Winter 43
Bonus activities 57

Hanukkah 59

Christmas 65
Bonus activities 78

Kwanzaa 79

New Year's Day 83

Martin Luther King Day 87

Chinese New Year 91

Groundhog Day 95

Valentine's Day 99
Bonus activities 110

Presidents' Day 111

Spring 115
Bonus activities 129

St. Patrick's Day 131

Easter 135
Bonus activities 144

Earth Day 145

Cinco de Mayo 149

Mother's Day 153

Summer 157
Bonus activities 168

Father's Day 169

Fourth of July 173

Fall

Note to the teacher: Have each child finish the picture by completing the tree and adding apples on the tree, under the tree, and in the squirrel's basket. Post the pictures with the title "Apples, Apples Everywhere!"

Seasonal Cards: Fall

TEC61202

TEC61202

TEC61202

TEC61202

TEC61202

TEC61202

Distracter Cards

TEC61202

TEC61202

TEC61202

Listen and Do

Color.

B

Note to the teacher: Provide oral directions, such as "Cross out the leaf" or "Color the small circle blue," for each child to follow. Then specify what you would like him to draw in the empty box at the bottom of the page.

Lots of Leaves

Color the matching leaves
in each row.

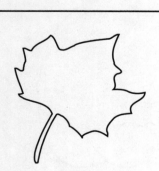

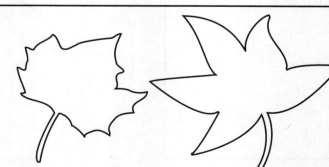

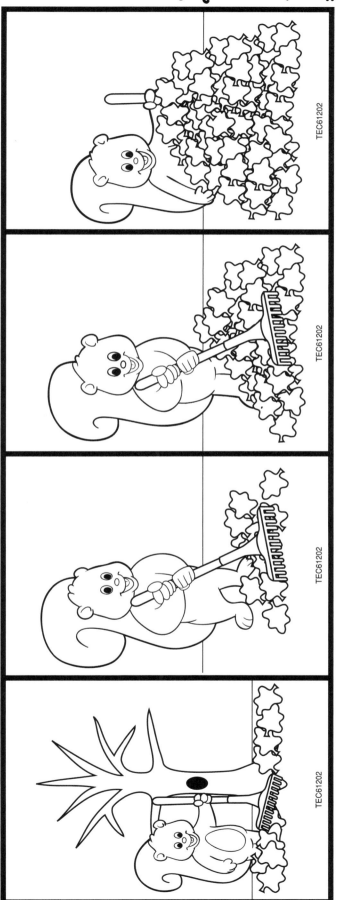

Math Mat: Copy and cut out the leaf and number cards from page 11. Use the mat and cards to provide a variety of hands-on math skill practice, including counting, number sets, comparing sets, number combinations, ordinal numbers, and odd and even numbers.

TEC61202	TEC61202	TEC61202	TEC61202	TEC61202
TEC61202	TEC61202	TEC61202	TEC61202	TEC61202
TEC61202	TEC61202	TEC61202	TEC61202	TEC61202
1	2	3	4	5
TEC61202	TEC61202	TEC61202	TEC61202	TEC61202
6	7	8	9	10
TEC61202	TEC61202	TEC61202	TEC61202	TEC61202
11	12	13	14	15
TEC61202	TEC61202	TEC61202	TEC61202	TEC61202

Name _____

P Is for Pumpkin

✂ Cut.

Glue the pictures that begin like 🎃.

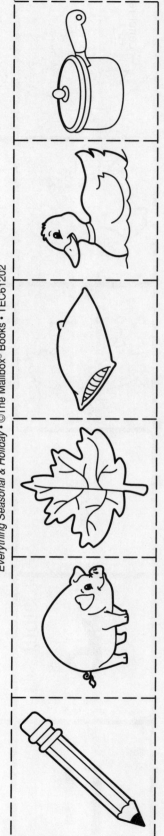

Everything Seasonal & Holiday • ©The Mailbox® Books • TEC61202

Name _____

Looking at Letters

✏ Circle the matching letters in each row.

🍁	l m t l l	
🎃	p k p s p	
🧹	a r r s r	

Hooray! It's Fall!
My favorite thing about fall is

by _____

Everything Seasonal & Holiday • ©The Mailbox® Books • TEC61202

Class Book Page: Have each child respond to the prompt orally (for you to write) or in writing. Then have her illustrate and personalize her work. Publish the pages in a class book titled "Favorite Fall Things."

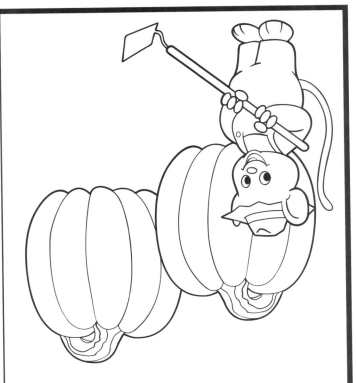

Five pumpkins.

Two pumpkins.

One fat pumpkin.

How Many Pumpkins?

Name _____

Fold-and-Go Booklet: To make a booklet, cut on the bold line. Fold along the thin horizontal line (keeping the programming to the outside) and then fold along the thin vertical line (keeping the cover to the outside).

15

Falling Leaves

Trace.

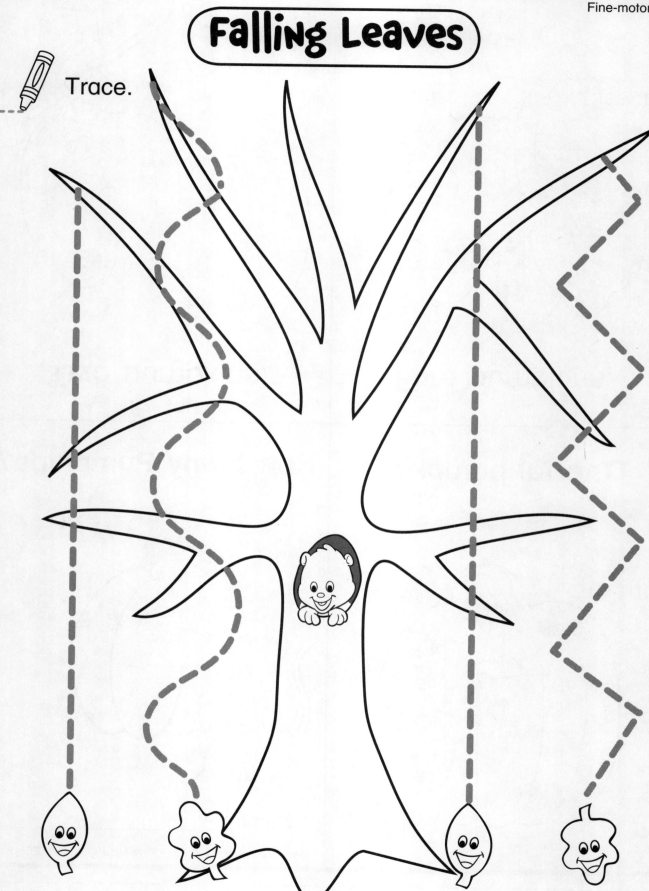

A Tasty Treat

Connect the dots in order from 1 to 10.

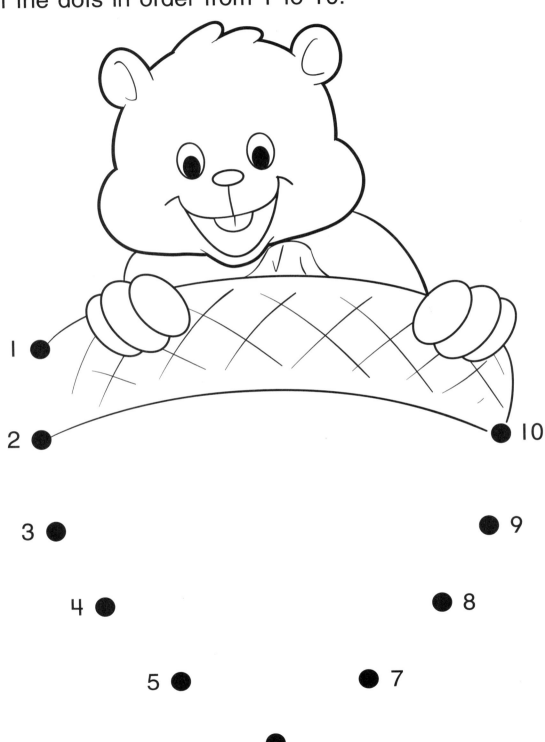

A Colorful Leaf

Materials: spray bottle of water, white construction paper, markers, scissors

Directions: Color the white paper all over with markers; then spray the paper lightly with water. Lay a copy of this page facedown on top of the wet paper and gently rub over the top of the paper. Turn the paper over and allow it to dry. Then cut on the bold line.

Finish the Picture

Center: Finish the tree on a copy of page 5; then color the tree and laminate it. Place the tree at a center along with orange, red, yellow, and brown play dough. A child rolls play dough into small balls to make colorful fall leaves to place on and around the tree. **Fine-motor skills**

Seasonal Cards

Individual: Make an accordion-folded book for each child by folding a 6" x 18" strip of construction paper into six sections. Label each section with a letter from the word *autumn* as shown. Each youngster colors and cuts out a copy of the seasonal cards from page 6 (discard the distracter cards). She glues one picture on each page of her booklet. Then she folds her booklet and takes it home to share what she's learned about autumn. **Making a book**

Math Mat and Manipulatives

Small group: To prepare, make a copy of the tree mat from page 10 on brown construction paper. Copy the cards from page 11 and number the leaf cards from 1 to 15. Cut out the cards. Place five number cards facedown on the tree with the matching leaf cards. A child turns over two cards. If they match, he keeps the cards. If they don't match, he turns them facedown again. Each child takes a turn in this manner until each pair of numbers has been matched. **Number matching**

Individual: For each child, program a copy of the tree mat from page 10 with blanks to equal the number of letters in her name. Then cut out several copies of the leaf cards on page 11. Write the letters in the child's name on the leaf cards, writing one uppercase letter on each card. Give each child her prepared tree mat and cards. The child places her cards facedown on her tree. She turns over a card, determines where the letter belongs in her name, and copies the letter in the corresponding blank. She continues in this manner until she has spelled her name. **Name spelling**

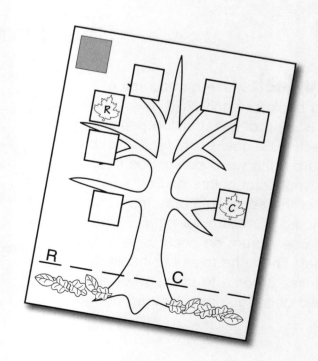

Grandparents Day

 loves

Note to the teacher: Have each child draw a picture of herself inside the heart and of her grandparent(s) on the bottom half of the paper. To make a card, fold the paper in half (keeping the artwork to the inside) and write "Happy Grandparents Day!" on the front.

Listen and Do

Draw.

Note to the teacher: Provide oral directions, such as "Cross off the picture that shows three cookies" or "Circle the letter *N*," for each child to follow. Then specify what you would like her to draw in the empty box at the bottom of the page.

You're the Best!

I love my _____ because

by _____

Everything Seasonal & Holiday • ©The Mailbox® Books • TEC61202

Class Book Page: Have each child respond to the prompt orally (for you to write) or in writing. Then have her illustrate and personalize her work. Publish the pages in a class book titled "Grandparents Are Special."

23

Name _____

Going to Grandma's House

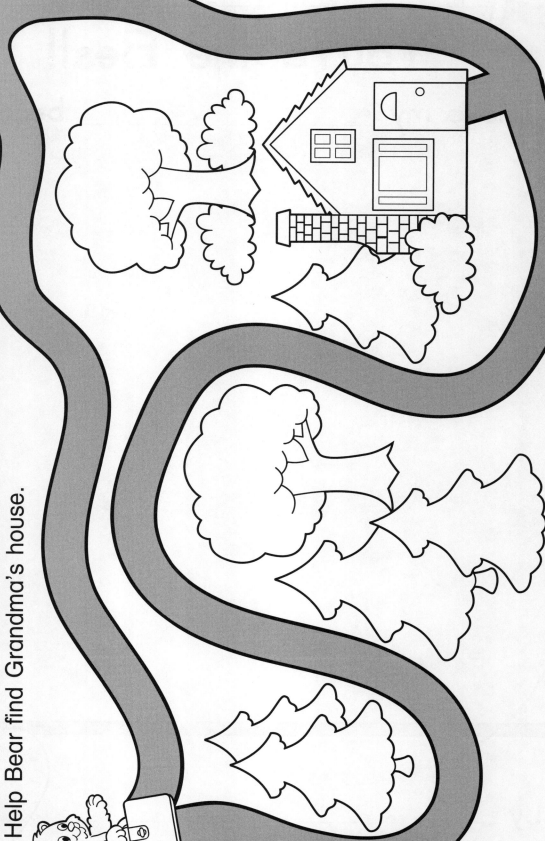

✏️ Draw.

Help Bear find Grandma's house.

Halloween

Note to the teacher: Have each child finish the picture by completing the pumpkin and then adding features to make it a jack-o'-lantern. Stack the pages and bind them into a class book titled "Jazzy Jack-o'-Lanterns!"

25

Name_____

Listen and Do

Draw.

Note to the teacher: Provide oral directions, such as "Cross off the bat" or "Color the pumpkin orange," for each child to follow. Then specify what you would like him to draw in the empty box at the bottom of the page.

Looking at Letters

✏️ Circle the matching letters in each row.

🎃	j	a	j	s	j	j
🕸️	p	w	w	w	s	w
🦇	b	b	b	x	o	b

Cat has **3** pieces of candy.

Spider has **2** pieces of candy.

Bat has **5** pieces of candy.

How Many Pieces?

Name _____

Everything Seasonal & Holiday • ©The Mailbox® Books • TEC61202

Fold-and-Go Booklet: To make a booklet, cut on the bold line. Fold along the thin horizontal line (keeping the programming to the outside) and then fold along the thin vertical line (keeping the cover to the outside).

Name_____

Just Hanging Around

Trace.

Everything Seasonal & Holiday • ©The Mailbox® Books • TEC61202

Note to the teacher: After the tracing is complete, have each child crumple small squares of black tissue paper and glue them to the spiders' bodies.

Quick Craft

TEC61202

Jolly Jack-o'-Lantern

Materials: orange tissue paper scraps, black and green construction paper scraps, glue, scissors

Directions: Tear the tissue paper scraps and glue them to the pumpkin. Then tear or cut from the black paper features to make a jack-o'-lantern and from the green paper a stem. Glue the features and stem in place. After the project is dry, cut along the bold line, trimming off any excess tissue paper.

Thanksgiving

Note to the teacher: Have each child finish the picture by adding feathers to the turkey. Then ask each child to imagine what a turkey might say if it could talk. Write each response in a speech bubble and attach it to the child's picture. Post the pictures with the title "If Turkeys Could Talk!"

Listen and Do

Draw.

Note to the teacher: Provide oral directions, such as "Color the big star yellow" or "Circle the corn," for each child to follow. Then specify what you would like her to draw in the empty box at the bottom of the page.

A Yummy Feast

Color the matching foods in each row.

   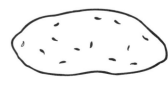

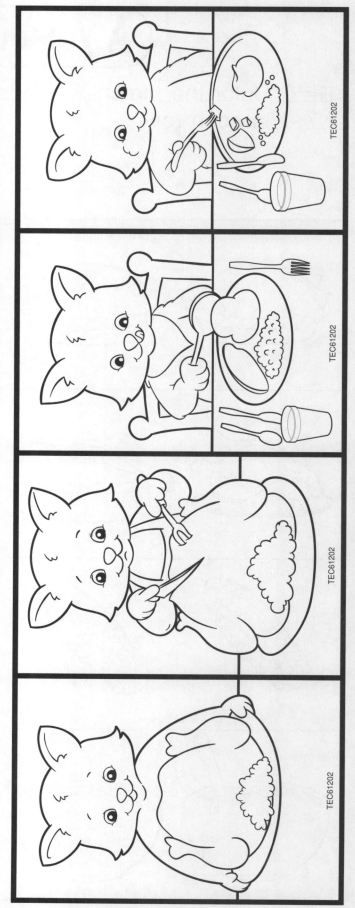

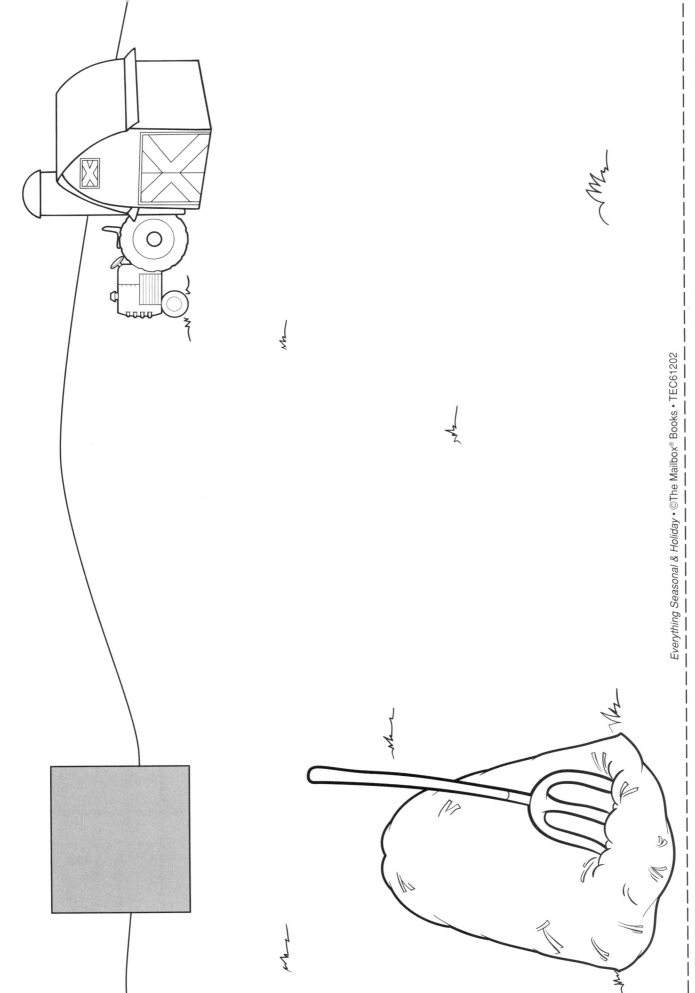

Everything Seasonal & Holiday • ©The Mailbox® Books • TEC61202

Math Mat: Copy and cut out the turkey and number cards from page 36. Use the mat and cards to provide a variety of hands-on math skill practice, including counting, number sets, comparing sets, number combinations, ordinal numbers, and odd and even numbers.

Turkey and Number Cards

Use with the math mat on page 35.

TEC61202	TEC61202	TEC61202	TEC61202	TEC61202
TEC61202	TEC61202	TEC61202	TEC61202	TEC61202
TEC61202	TEC61202	TEC61202	TEC61202	TEC61202
1	2	3	4	5
TEC61202	TEC61202	TEC61202	TEC61202	TEC61202
6	7	8	9	10
TEC61202	TEC61202	TEC61202	TEC61202	TEC61202
11	12	13	14	15
TEC61202	TEC61202	TEC61202	TEC61202	TEC61202

T is for Turkey

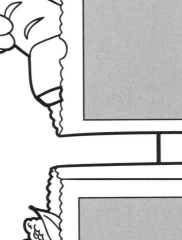

✂ Cut.

Glue the pictures that begin like 🦃.

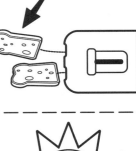

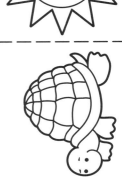
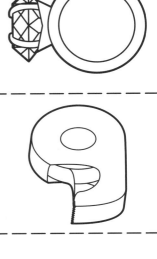

Everything Seasonal & Holiday • ©The Mailbox® Books • TEC61202

37

Name _____

Looking at Letters

✏ Circle the matching letters in each row.

c	m	c	b	c c
t	t	v	j	t
d	f	f	f	n

Everything Seasonal & Holiday • ©The Mailbox® Books • TEC61202

It's Thanksgiving Day!

On Thanksgiving Day, I like to

by _____

Everything Seasonal & Holiday • ©The Mailbox® Books • TEC61202

Class Book Page: Have each child respond to the prompt orally (for you to write) or in writing. Then have her illustrate and personalize her work. Publish the pages in a class book titled "On Thanksgiving Day."

39

Name _____

Ready to Eat

Trace.

TEC61202

Turkey's Colorful Feathers

Materials: four 6" x 9" sheets of white construction paper, several shallow containers of different-colored paint, sponges, scissors, glue

Directions: Sponge-paint each sheet of paper a different color. After the paint is dry, trim each piece of paper into a feather shape. Color the turkey and then cut on the bold line. Finally, glue the feathers on the turkey.

Bonus Activities

Math Mat and Manipulatives

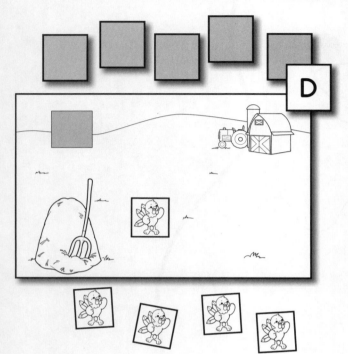

Small group: Give each child a copy of the math mat from page 35 along with a copy of the turkey cards on page 36, cut apart. (Set the number cards aside for another use.) To play Turkey Wobble, spread a set of alphabet cards facedown on the table. In turn, each child picks a card and names the letter. If he is correct, he wobbles one of his turkeys onto his mat and sets the letter card aside. If he is incorrect, he places the letter card facedown on the table again. Play continues in the same manner until each child has wobbled all his turkey cards onto his mat. **Letter identification**

Quick Craft

Large group: Place an enlarged copy of the turkey pattern from page 41 in your group area along with a class supply of colorful construction paper feathers. To begin, have youngsters say the word *turkey* several times, emphasizing the beginning sound. Next, invite a volunteer to name a word that has the same beginning sound as *turkey.* After confirming that the word does begin with the /t/ sound, have her place a feather on the turkey. Continue until each child has had the opportunity to add a feather to the turkey. **Beginning sound /t/**

Winter

Note to the teacher: Have each child finish the picture by completing the snowpal and adding wintry details that may include a picture of himself dressed in winter clothing. Post the pictures with the title "Welcome, Winter!"

Seasonal Cards: Winter

Distracter Cards

Everything Seasonal & Holiday • ©The Mailbox® Books • TEC61202

Listen and Do

Draw.

Note to the teacher: Provide oral directions, such as "Circle the spoon" or "Color the square red," for each child to follow. Then specify what you would like her to draw in the empty box at the bottom of the page.

Matching Mittens

Color the matching mittens in each row.

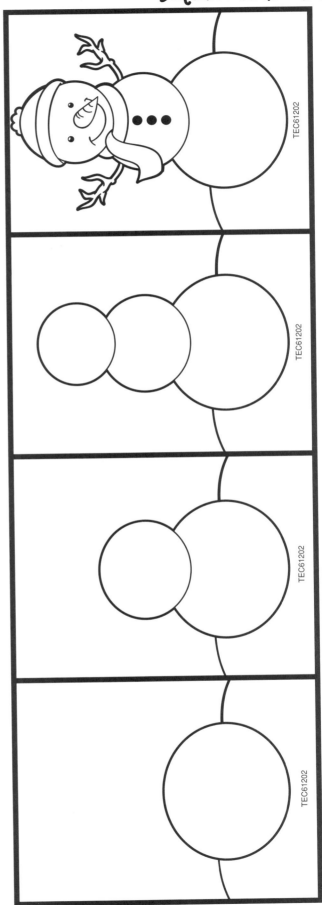

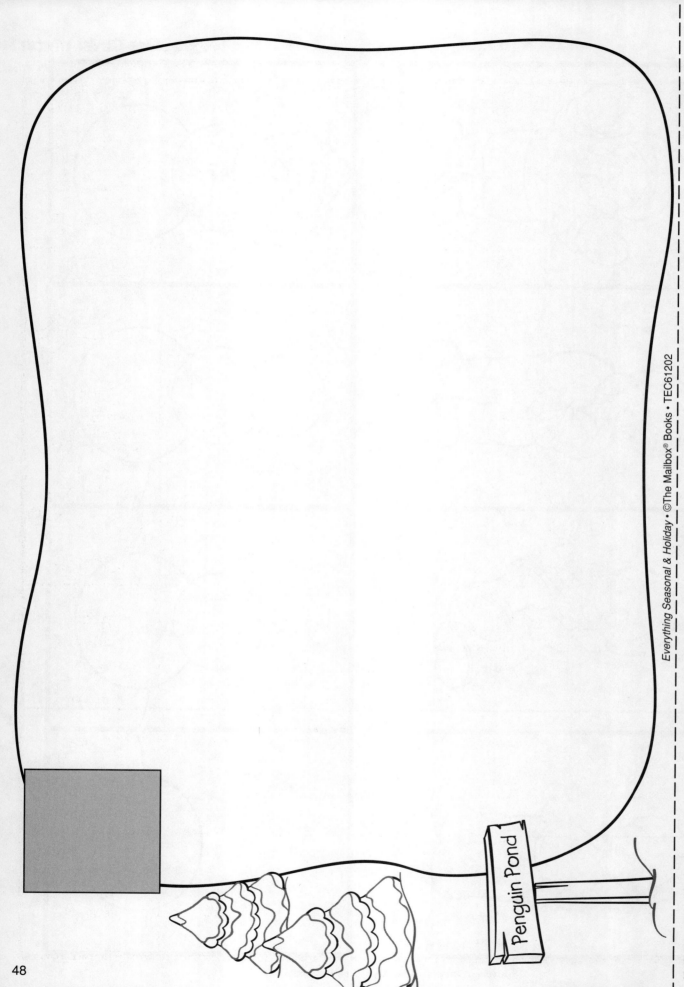

Penguin Pond

48

Everything Seasonal & Holiday • ©The Mailbox® Books • TEC61202

Math Mat: Copy and cut out the penguin and number cards from page 49. Use the mat and cards to provide a variety of hands-on math skill practice, including counting, number sets, comparing sets, number combinations, ordinal numbers, and odd and even numbers.

TEC61202	TEC61202	TEC61202	TEC61202	TEC61202
TEC61202	TEC61202	TEC61202	TEC61202	TEC61202
TEC61202	TEC61202	TEC61202	TEC61202	TEC61202
1 TEC61202	**2** TEC61202	**3** TEC61202	**4** TEC61202	**5** TEC61202
6 TEC61202	**7** TEC61202	**8** TEC61202	**9** TEC61202	**10** TEC61202
11 TEC61202	**12** TEC61202	**13** TEC61202	**14** TEC61202	**15** TEC61202

Name

M Is for Mitten

Cut.

Glue the pictures that begin like .

Looking at Letters

Circle the matching letters in each row.

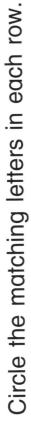

h	h	l	h	s
e	m	s	m	m
b	b	f	b	b

Brrrr!
When I feel cold in the wintertime,

by _____

Class Book Page: Have each child respond to the prompt orally (for you to write) or in writing. Then have him illustrate and personalize his work. Publish the pages in a class book titled "Keeping Warm This Winter."

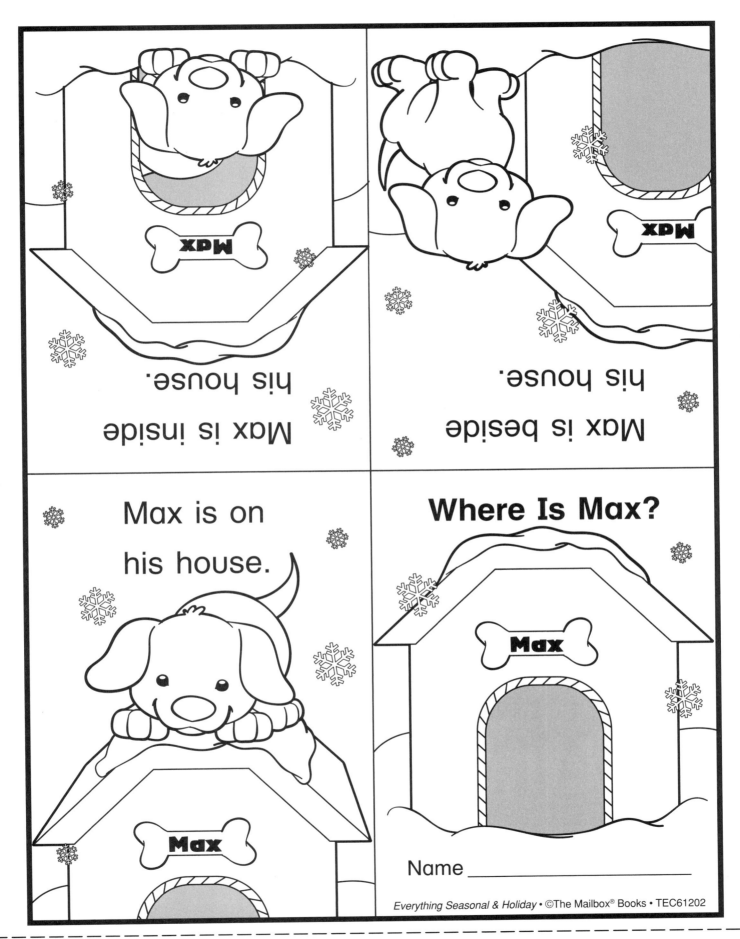

Max is inside
his house.

Max is beside
his house.

Max is on
his house.

Where Is Max?

Max

Name _____

Everything Seasonal & Holiday • ©The Mailbox® Books • TEC61202

Fold-and-Go Booklet: To make a booklet, cut on the bold line. Fold along the thin horizontal line (keeping the programming to the outside) and then fold along the thin vertical line (keeping the cover to the outside).

53

Pretty Snowflake

Trace.

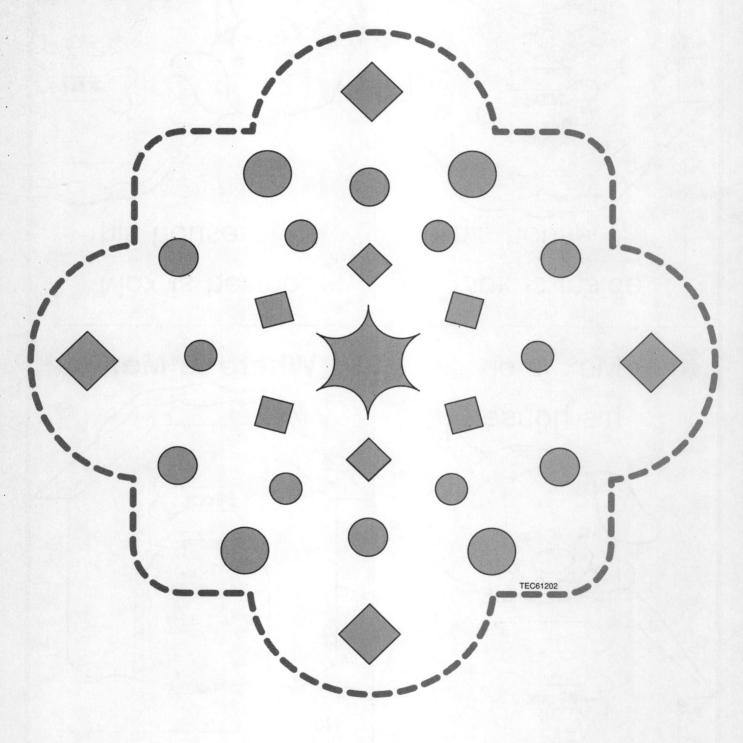

TEC61202

Note to the teacher: For a snowflake art project, copy this page on light blue construction paper. Have a child trace around the shape 54 and then cut it out. Finally, have her use a large sponge piece to dab glitter-embellished glue on the cutout.

Time for Cocoa

 Draw.

Help Penguin find the hot cocoa.

Quick Craft

A Winter Home for Squirrel

Materials: 9" x 12" sheet of brown construction paper with corners trimmed; nest-making materials, such as yarn or string pieces, polyester stuffing, or paper scraps; crayons; scissors; glue

Directions: Color the squirrel and then cut on the bold line. Glue the cutout to the center of the construction paper. Glue an assortment of nest-making materials around the squirrel to make a nest that appears warm and cozy.

Bonus Activities

Seasonal Cards

Individual: Write *Winter* across the top of a sheet of paper and copy the sheet to make a class supply. Also copy a class supply of the seasonal and distracter cards from page 44. Each youngster colors and cuts out a set of cards. She chooses a card and determines if the picture shown is related to winter. If it is, she glues it onto her paper. If it is not, she sets it aside. She continues in this manner with each remaining card. **Sorting**

Fine-Motor Practice Page

Center: Laminate a dark blue construction paper copy of page 54 and place it at a center along with a supply of white play dough mixed with silver glitter. A child rolls play dough into snake shapes and uses them to form the snowflake on the page. **Fine-motor skills**

Name_____

Trace.

Pretty Snowflake

Winter
Fine-motor skills

Math Mat and Manipulatives

Small group: To prepare, copy the math mat on page 48 and cut out a copy of the penguin cards on page 49. Show the math mat and one penguin card to the group. Ask each child to estimate the number of penguin cards that will fit inside the pond without overlapping. Record each youngster's guess on the board. Then have the group help you place penguins inside the pond. When the pond is full, lead the group in counting the penguins. Then have each child compare his estimate to the actual number of penguins that fit inside the pond. **Estimation**

Large group: Cut apart one copy of the number cards from page 49 and make a class supply of the penguin cards on page 49. Also copy the math mat on page 48. To begin, hold up a number card. Help a student volunteer identify the number; then invite her to place a penguin in (or around) the pond. Continue in this manner, shuffling and reusing the number cards as needed, until each child has had a turn. **Number identification**

Eight.

Hanukkah

Note to the teacher: Have each child finish the picture by completing the candles and gluing a flame (a small piece of crumpled yellow tissue paper) to the top of each candle. Post the pictures with the title "Marvelous Menorahs!"

Name_____

Listen and Do

Draw.

Everything Seasonal & Holiday • ©The Mailbox® Books • TEC61202

60 **Note to the teacher:** Provide oral directions, such as "Cross out the potato" or "Color the teddy bear blue," for each child to follow. Then specify what you would like her to draw in the empty box at the bottom of the page.

Name

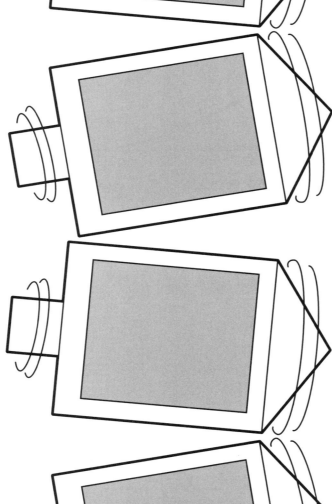

H Is for Hat

Cut.

Glue the pictures that begin like 🎩.

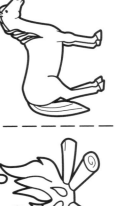

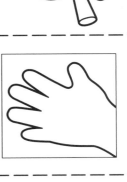

Everything Seasonal & Holiday • ©The Mailbox® Books • TEC61202

61

ladle.

rhymes with

Dreidel

sandal.

rhymes with

Candle

Star

rhymes with

car.

Hanukkah Rhymes

Name _____

Everything Seasonal & Holiday • ©The Mailbox® Books • TEC61202

Fold-and-Go Booklet: To make a booklet, cut on the bold line. Fold along the thin horizontal line (keeping the programming to the outside) and then fold along the thin vertical line (keeping the cover to the outside).

Name _____

Spin the Dreidel

Connect the dots in order from 1 to 10.

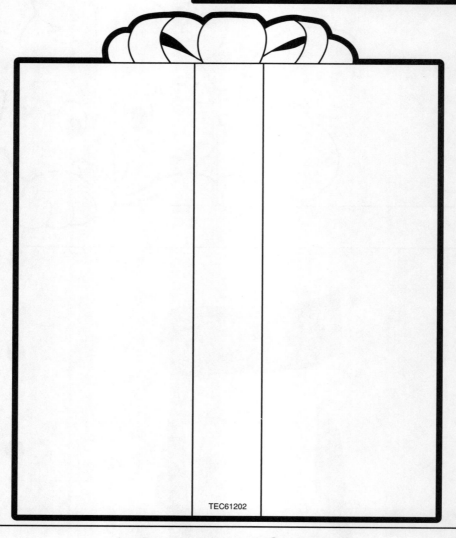

TEC61202

A Gorgeous Gift Card

Materials: 9" x 12" sheet of construction paper folded in half horizontally (card), white corn syrup tinted with blue or yellow food coloring, sponge, silver or gold glitter, scissors, glue

Directions: Sponge-paint the gift box with the corn syrup and then sprinkle it with glitter. After the gift box is dry, cut along the bold line; then glue the gift box to the front of the card. Attach a signed gift tag cutout. Finally, write a message to the recipient inside the card.

Christmas

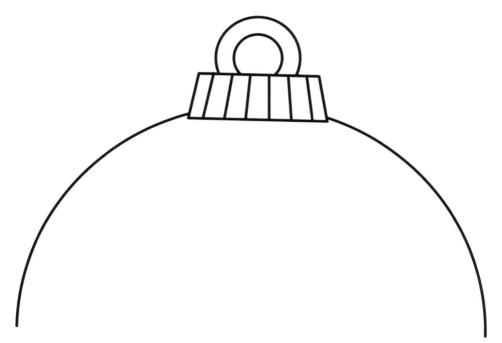

Note to the teacher: Have each child finish the picture by completing the ornament and decorating it as desired. Cut out each ornament and hang it on a large Christmas tree cutout. Title the display "Trimming the Tree!"

Listen and Do

Draw.

Note to the teacher: Provide oral directions, such as "Color the gingerbread girl" or "Cross off the letter *C*," for each child to follow. Then specify what you would like him to draw in the empty box at the bottom of the page.

Christmas Match

Color the matching pictures in each row.

  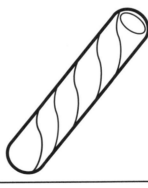 

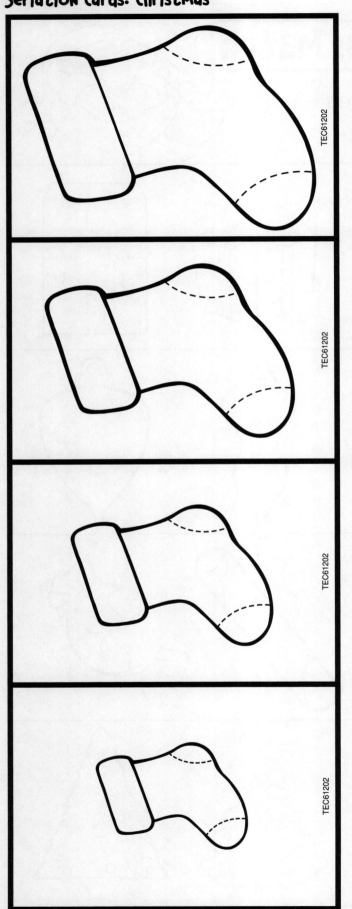

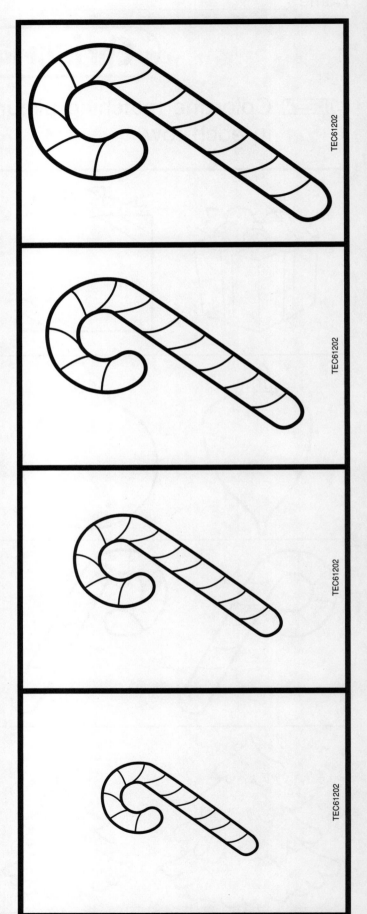

Everything Seasonal & Holiday • ©The Mailbox® Books • TEC61202

Math Mat: Copy and cut out the ornament and number cards from page 70. Use the mat and cards to provide a variety of hands-on math skill practice, including counting, number sets, comparing sets, number combinations, ordinal numbers, and odd and even numbers.

Ornament and Number Cards
Use with the math mat on page 69.

TEC61202	TEC61202	TEC61202	TEC61202	TEC61202
TEC61202	TEC61202	TEC61202	TEC61202	TEC61202
TEC61202	TEC61202	TEC61202	TEC61202	TEC61202
1	2	3	4	5
TEC61202	TEC61202	TEC61202	TEC61202	TEC61202
6	7	8	9	10
TEC61202	TEC61202	TEC61202	TEC61202	TEC61202
11	12	13	14	15
TEC61202	TEC61202	TEC61202	TEC61202	TEC61202

Everything Seasonal & Holiday • ©The Mailbox® Books • TEC61202

Name _____

R Is for Reindeer

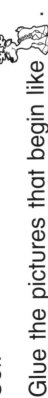

Cut.

Glue the pictures that begin like .

Everything Seasonal & Holiday • ©The Mailbox® Books • TEC61202

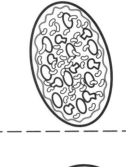

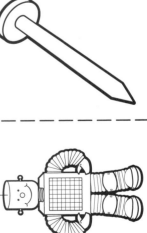

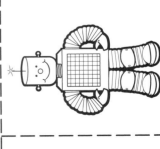

71

Name _____

Looking at Letters

 Circle the matching letters in each row.

	l	s	w	l	l
	g	g	z	a	g	u
	w	r	c	r	r	r

Christmas Is Special

Christmas is a special time because

by _____

Everything Seasonal & Holiday • ©The Mailbox® Books • TEC61202

Class Book Page: Have each child respond to the prompt orally (for you to write) or in writing. Then have him illustrate and personalize his work. Publish the pages in a class book titled "We Love Christmas!"

Santa is **on** the roof.

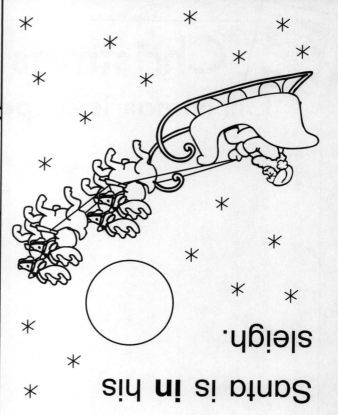

Santa is **in** his sleigh.

Santa is **behind** the tree.

Where Is Santa?

Name _____

Fold-and-Go Booklet: To make a booklet, cut on the bold line. Fold along the thin horizontal line (keeping the programming to the outside) and then fold along the thin vertical line (keeping the cover to the outside).

A Beautiful Wreath

Crumple.

 Glue.

Note to the teacher: Have each child crumple green tissue paper squares and glue them to the wreath. Then have him crumple a few red tissue paper squares and glue them to the wreath so they resemble berries.

Santa's Hat

Connect the dots in order from 1 to 10.

Everything Seasonal & Holiday • ©The Mailbox® Books • TEC61202

TEC61202

Adorable Gingerbread Pal

Materials: 9" x 12" sheet of brown construction paper; various craft materials, such as colorful paper scraps, rickrack, pom-poms, and yarn; scissors; glue

Directions: Trace a copy of the gingerbread person onto the brown paper and cut it out. Then use the various craft materials to decorate the cutout as desired.

Math Mat and Manipulatives

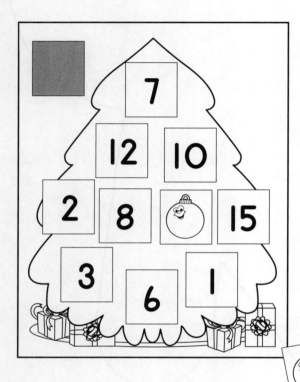

Small Group: For each group member, make a lotto board by randomly gluing ten number cards (use copies of the cards from page 70) on a copy of the math mat from page 69. Cut out an additional set of the number cards and place them in a container. Give each child in the group ten ornament cards (copied from page 70) to use as markers. To play, take a card from the container and say the number aloud. If a child has the corresponding number on his board, he covers it with a marker. Play continues until each player has covered all the numbers on his board. **Number recognition**

Seriation Cards

Small Group: Help each child cut out a copy of the stocking seriation cards on page 68. Have her glue the cards in order from smallest to largest on a sheet of green construction paper. Finally, have her glue a small candy cane above each stocking. **One-to-one correspondence**

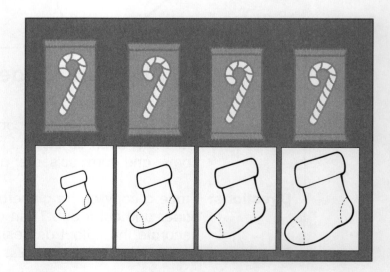

Kwanzaa

Everything Seasonal & Holiday • ©The Mailbox® Books • TEC61202

Note to the teacher: Have each child finish the picture by completing the bowl; then have her cut pictures of fruits and vegetables from a magazine and glue them to the top of the bowl to symbolize the mazao (crops). Mount the pictures on a large sheet of bulletin board paper decorated so it resembles a placemat and add the title "Celebrating Kwanzaa."

Name _____

Listen and Do

Draw.

Everything Seasonal & Holiday • ©The Mailbox® Books • TEC61202

Note to the teacher: Provide oral directions, such as "Color the apple green" or "Circle the number nine," for each child to follow. Then specify what you would like her to draw in the empty box at the bottom of the page.

A Delicious Feast!

At a Kwanzaa feast, I would serve

by _____

Class Book Page: Have each child respond to the prompt orally (for you to write) or in writing. Then have her illustrate and personalize her work. Publish the pages in a class book titled "A Kwanzaa Feast."

Quick Craft

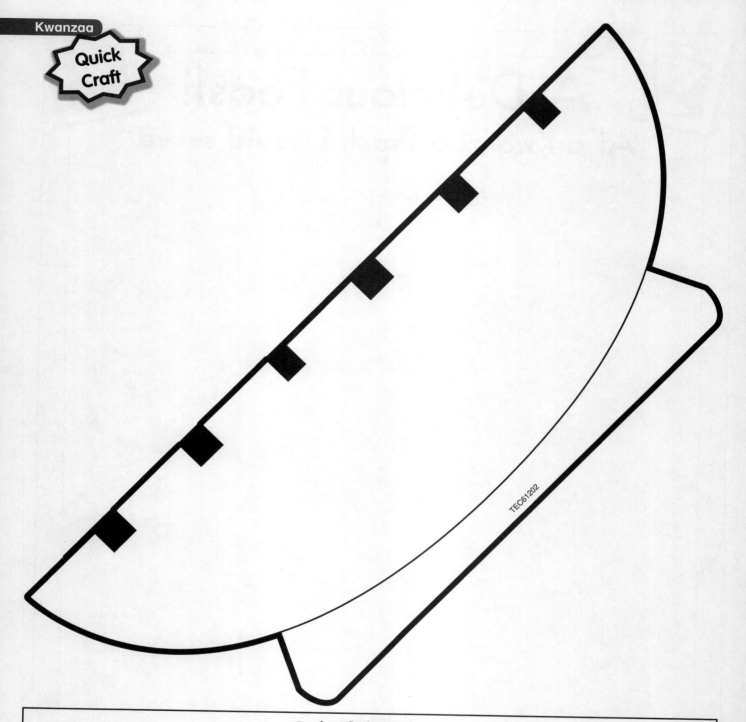

TEC61202

Colorful Kinara

Materials: 9" x12" sheet of construction paper; 7 craft sticks; red, black, and green tempera paint; yellow tissue paper squares; paintbrush; crayons; scissors; glue

Directions: Color the kinara and then cut along the bold line. Glue the cutout near the bottom of the construction paper. Next, paint three craft sticks red, three green, and the remaining one black. After the paint is dry, glue the craft sticks above the kinara so they resemble candles. (Glue the black craft stick in the center, the red craft sticks on one side of the black, and the green craft sticks on the other side.) Finally, glue a crumpled tissue paper square to the top of each craft stick so it resembles a flame.

New Year's Day

Everything Seasonal & Holiday • ©The Mailbox® Books • TEC61202

Note to the teacher: Have each child finish the picture by completing the hat and decorating it as desired. Post the pictures with the title "Happy New Year!"

Listen and Do

Draw.

Note to the teacher: Provide oral directions, such as "Color the balloons" or "Cross off the letter *B*," for each child to follow. Then specify what you would like him to draw in the empty box at the bottom of the page.

A Brand-New Year!

This year, I would like to

by _____

Everything Seasonal & Holiday • ©The Mailbox® Books • TEC61202

Class Book Page: Have each child respond to the prompt orally (for you to write) or in writing. Then have him illustrate and personalize his work. Publish the pages in a class book titled "A Brand-New Year."

Name _____

A Banner Year!

Cut.

Happy New Year!

Martin Luther King Day

Note to the teacher: Have each child finish the picture by completing the dove and gluing white craft feathers to the wing and tail. Post the pictures with the title "Dreaming of Peace."

Name_____

Listen and Do

Draw.

Everything Seasonal & Holiday • ©The Mailbox® Books • TEC61202

Note to the teacher: Provide oral directions, such as "Color the rectangle red" or "Cross out the number ten," for each child to follow. Then specify what you would like her to draw in the empty box at the bottom of the page.

He wanted people to
be nice to each other.

Martin Luther King Jr.
had a dream.

He wanted people to
work together.

Martin Luther King Jr.

Name _____

Everything Seasonal & Holiday • ©The Mailbox® Books • TEC61202

Fold-and-Go Booklet: To make a booklet, cut on the bold line. Fold along the thin horizontal line (keeping the programming to the outside) and then fold along the thin vertical line (keeping the cover to the outside).

Peace Dove

Connect the dots in order from 1 to 15.

Chinese New Year

Everything Seasonal & Holiday • ©The Mailbox® Books • TEC61202

Note to the teacher: Have each child finish the picture by completing the sparklers and drawing fireworks in the sky. If desired, invite youngsters to decorate the fireworks with glitter. Bind the pictures into a class booked titled "A Sparkling Celebration!"

91

Name_____

Listen and Do

Draw.

Everything Seasonal & Holiday • ©The Mailbox® Books • TEC61202

Note to the teacher: Provide oral directions, such as "Cross off the number 12" or "Circle the lowercase *r*," for each child to follow. Then specify what you would like him to draw in the empty box at the bottom of the page.

Lion has **six** pennies.

Lion has **three** pennies.

Lion has **eight** pennies.

Lion's Lucky Money

Gung Hay Fat Choy!

Name _____

Everything Seasonal & Holiday • ©The Mailbox® Books • TEC61202

Fold-and-Go Booklet: To make a booklet, cut on the bold line. Fold along the thin horizontal line (keeping the programming to the outside) and then fold along the thin vertical line (keeping the cover to the outside).

TEC61202

Decorative Windsock

Materials: 9" x 12" sheet of red construction paper, 12" red construction paper strip, colorful crepe paper streamers, markers, stapler, scissors, glue

Directions: Color the dragon and cut out the scroll. Glue the cutout to the center of the construction paper and decorate as desired. Staple the paper into a cylinder shape (keeping the cutout to the outside). Then staple the paper strip to the top of the cylinder to make a handle. Finally, glue crepe paper streamers to the bottom of the resulting windsock.

Groundhog Day

Note to the teacher: Have each child finish the picture by completing the groundhog. If desired, have youngsters tear black paper scraps and glue them to the groundhog's shadow. Post the pictures with the title "Is It Spring Yet?"

Name _____

Listen and Do

Draw.

Note to the teacher: Provide oral directions, such as "Cross off the number 11" or "Circle the uppercase *G*," for each child to follow. Then specify what you would like her to draw in the empty box at the bottom of the page.

What Will Happen?

When the groundhog comes out of its burrow,

by _____

Class Book Page: Have each child respond to the prompt orally (for you to write) or in writing. Then have her illustrate and personalize her work. Publish the pages in a class book titled "Groundhog's Surprise!"

Back to Bed!

Draw.
Help Groundhog find his bed.

Valentine's Day

Note to the teacher: Have each child finish the picture by completing the heart and decorating it for Valentine's Day. Help each child cut out the heart; then have him glue it to a sheet of folded construction paper and decorate the resulting card as desired. Finally, have him write on the card, or dictate for you to write, a special message to the recipient.

Listen and Do

Draw.

Note to the teacher: Provide oral directions, such as "Circle the lowercase *v*" or "Color the big heart purple," for each child to follow. Then specify what you would like him to draw in the empty box at the bottom of the page.

Heart-to-Heart

Color the matching hearts in each row.

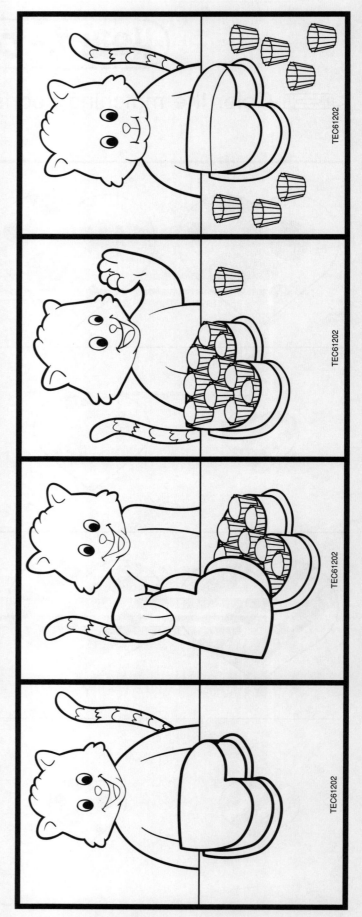

Everything Seasonal & Holiday • ©The Mailbox® Books • TEC61202

Math Mat: Copy and cut out the cookie and number cards from page 104. Use the mat and the cards to provide a variety of hands-on math skill practice, including counting, number sets, comparing sets, number combinations, ordinal numbers, and odd and even numbers.

TEC61202	TEC61202	TEC61202	TEC61202	TEC61202
TEC61202	TEC61202	TEC61202	TEC61202	TEC61202
TEC61202	TEC61202	TEC61202	TEC61202	TEC61202
1 TEC61202	2 TEC61202	3 TEC61202	4 TEC61202	5 TEC61202
6 TEC61202	7 TEC61202	8 TEC61202	9 TEC61202	10 TEC61202
11 TEC61202	12 TEC61202	13 TEC61202	14 TEC61202	15 TEC61202

V Is for Valentine

 Cut.

Glue the pictures that begin like .

Looking at Letters

Circle the matching letters in each row.

	h	d	h	h	k
	q	l	e	l	l
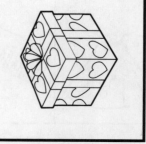	a	g	g	x	g

A Special Valentine Message

On Valentine's Day, I would like to say

by _____

Class Book Page: Have each child respond to the prompt orally (for you to write) or in writing. Then have him illustrate and personalize his work. Publish the pages in a class book titled "Special Valentine Messages."

Puppy Love

✎ Draw.
Help Puppy find his valentine.

I love you.

Happy Valentine's Day!

Quick Craft

TEC61202

Valentine Pop-Up Card

Materials: tagboard template of the heart, 12" x 18" sheet of construction paper folded in half, 1" x 6" strip of construction paper, child's photo glued to a 3" heart cutout, tape, crayons, scissors

Directions: Place the tagboard heart along the fold of the construction paper. Trace around the heart; then cut it out, leaving the fold intact. Decorate the front of the card as desired. Accordion-fold the strip. Tape one end of the strip to the photo; then open the card and tape the remaining end of the strip to the inside of the card. Finally, write a valentine message inside the card.

Math Mat and Manipulatives

Eight.

Small Group: Give each student a copy of page 103 and a set of the cookie cards from page 104. Cut apart a copy of the number cards from page 104 and place them in a container. Pick a card from the container and say the number aloud. Each student places a corresponding number of cookie cards on his cookie sheet. Then he quietly counts the cookies. Each child removes the cards from his cookie sheet and play continues until each number has been called. **Counting**

Maze

Individual: Give each student a copy of page 108. Provide youngsters with glue and several different colors of glitter. A child squeezes a line of glue on a path and then sprinkles one color of glitter on the glue. She repeats the process with different-colored glitter for each additional path she finds. **Spatial sense**

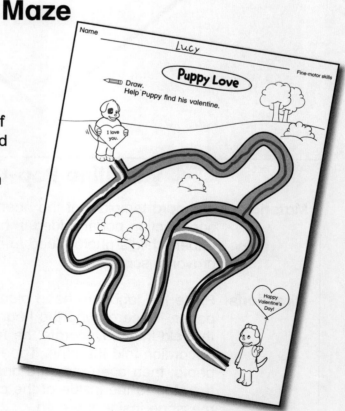

Name _____
Lucy

Puppy Love

Fine-motor skills

Draw.
Help Puppy find his valentine.

I love you.

Happy Valentine's Day!

Presidents' Day

Note to the teacher: Have each child finish the picture by adding logs to the cabin. If desired, have each child tear strips of brown construction paper and glue them to the cabin so they resemble logs.

Name_____

Listen and Do

Draw.

Note to the teacher: Provide oral directions, such as "Cross out the lowercase *a*" or "Color the big diamond orange," for each child to follow. Then specify what you would like her to draw in the empty box at the bottom of the page.

The **quarter** shows George Washington.

Kitty has a **quarter** and a **penny.**

The **penny** shows Abraham Lincoln.

Kitty's Coins

Name _____

Fold-and-Go Booklet: To make a booklet, cut on the bold line. Fold along the thin horizontal line (keeping the programming to the outside) and then fold along the thin vertical line (keeping the cover to the outside).

A Big Hat!

Connect the dots in order from 1 to 15.

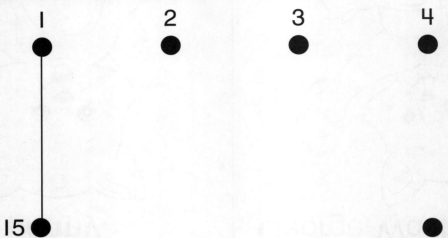

Spring

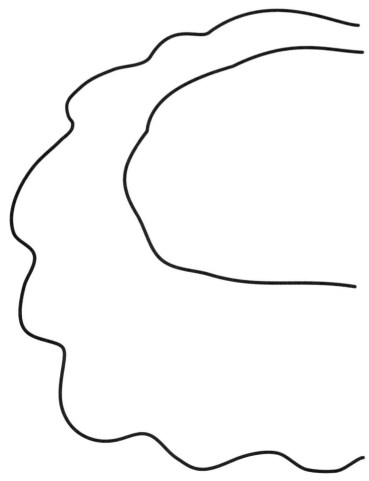

Note to the teacher: Have each child finish the picture by completing the nest and adding eggs and/or a bird to the nest. Post the pictures with the title "What's in the Nest?"

Seasonal Cards: Spring

TEC61202

TEC61202

TEC61202

TEC61202

TEC61202

TEC61202

Distracter Cards

TEC61202

TEC61202

TEC61202

Listen and Do

Draw.

Note to the teacher: Provide oral directions, such as "Circle the ladybug" or "Color the heart red," for each child to follow. Then specify what you would like him to draw in the empty box at the bottom of the page.

Name_____

Colorful Flowers

Color the matching flowers in each row.

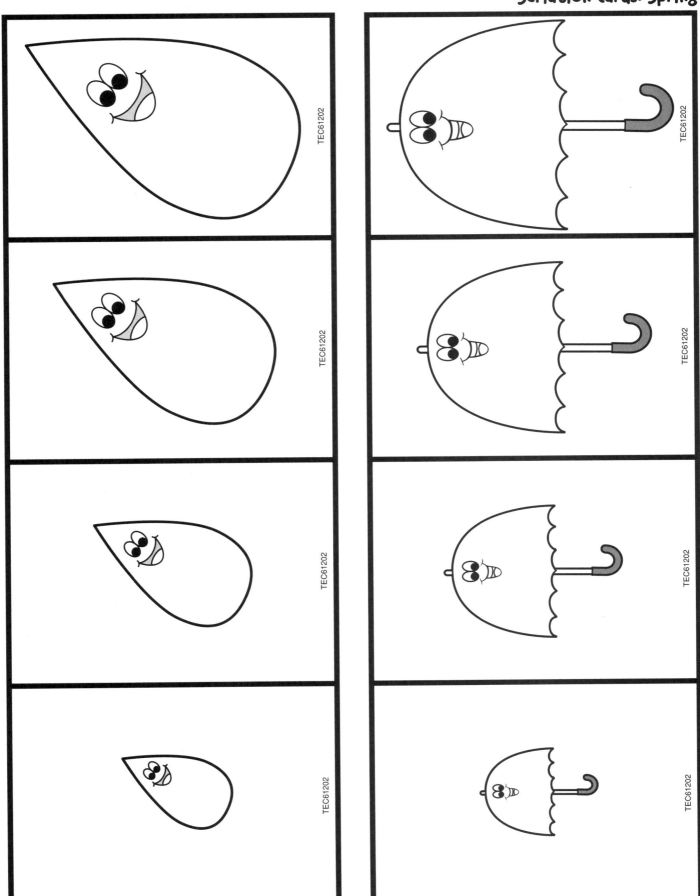

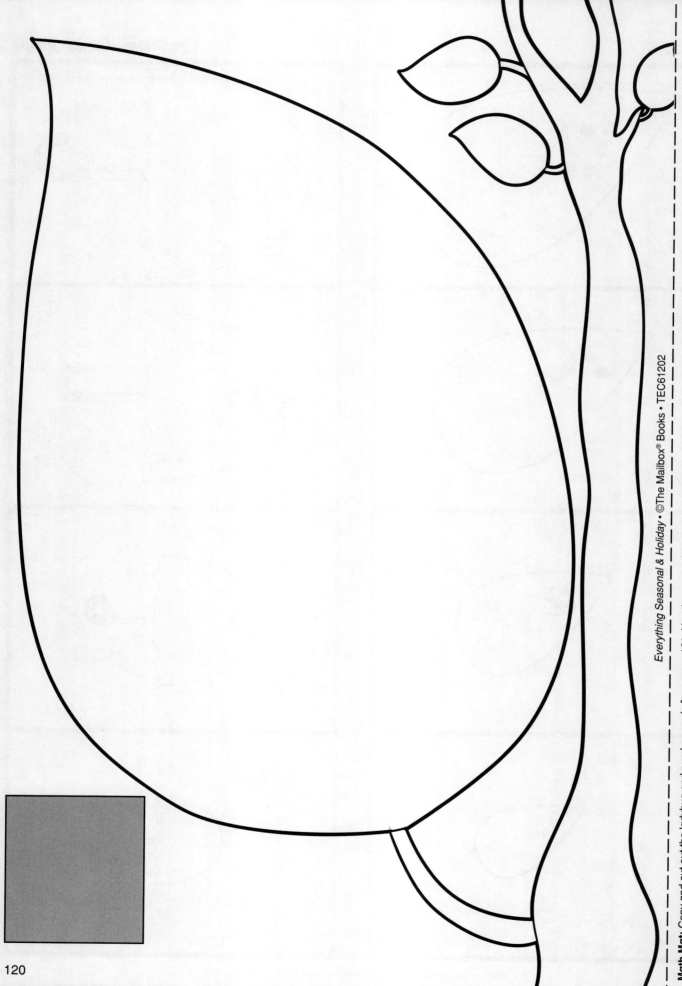

Everything Seasonal & Holiday • ©The Mailbox® Books • TEC61202

Math Mat: Copy and cut out the ladybug and number cards from page 121. Use the mat and cards to provide a variety of hands-on math skill practice, including counting, number sets, comparing sets, number combinations, ordinal numbers, and odd and even numbers.

TEC61202	TEC61202	TEC61202	TEC61202	TEC61202
TEC61202	TEC61202	TEC61202	TEC61202	TEC61202
TEC61202	TEC61202	TEC61202	TEC61202	TEC61202
1	**2**	**3**	**4**	**5**
TEC61202	TEC61202	TEC61202	TEC61202	TEC61202
6	**7**	**8**	**9**	**10**
TEC61202	TEC61202	TEC61202	TEC61202	TEC61202
11	**12**	**13**	**14**	**15**
TEC61202	TEC61202	TEC61202	TEC61202	TEC61202

B Is for Butterfly

Cut.

Glue the pictures that begin like 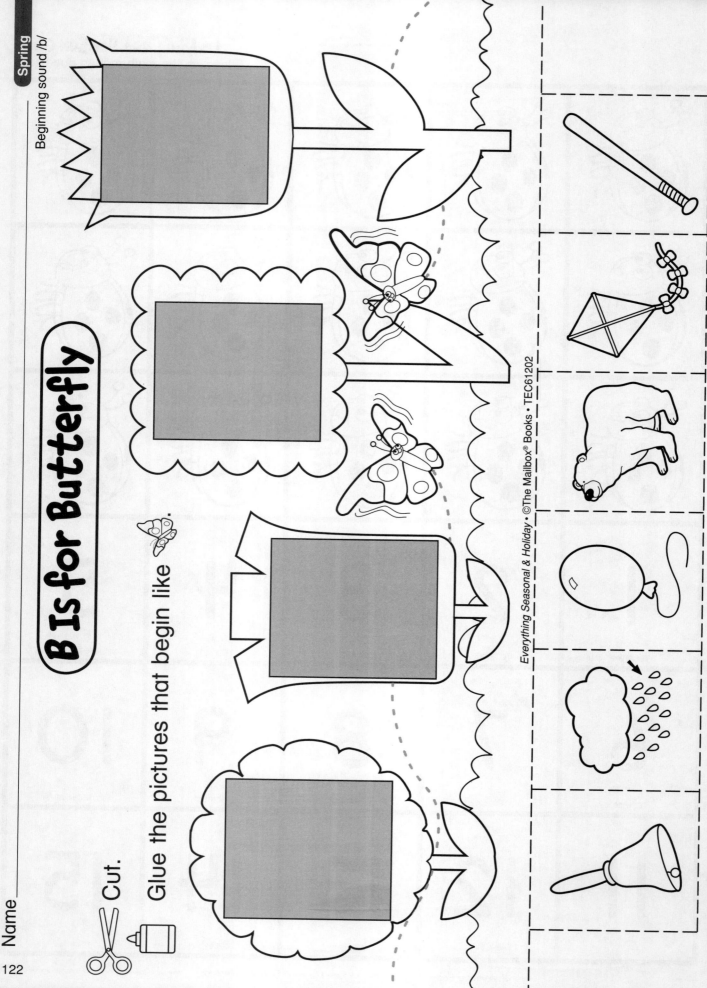.

Everything Seasonal & Holiday • ©The Mailbox® Books • TEC61202

Name _____

Looking at Letters

✏️ Circle the matching letters in each row.

t	t	r	r	s	r
b	b	b	m	b	f
g	g	n	n	u	p	n

Splish, Splash!
On a rainy spring day, I like to

by _____

Class Book Page: Have each child respond to the prompt orally (for you to write) or in writing. Then have him illustrate and personalize his work. Publish the pages in a class book titled "Rainy Day Fun."

ƃnqʎpɐl ɹoɟ sı **⅂**

˙ʞɔnp ɹoɟ sı **ᗡ**

R is for rain.

My Spring Beginning Sounds Booklet

Name _____

Fold-and-Go Booklet: To make a booklet, cut on the bold line. Fold along the thin horizontal line (keeping the programming to the outside) and then fold along the thin vertical line (keeping the cover to the outside).

High-Flying Fun

 Cut.

Glue.

Everything Seasonal & Holiday • ©The Mailbox® Books • TEC61202

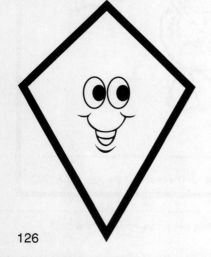

Rainy Weather

Connect the dots in order from 1 to 10.

4 ●

3 ●

5 ●

2 ●

6 ●

10 ●

8 ●

1 ●

7 ●

9 ●

Quick Craft

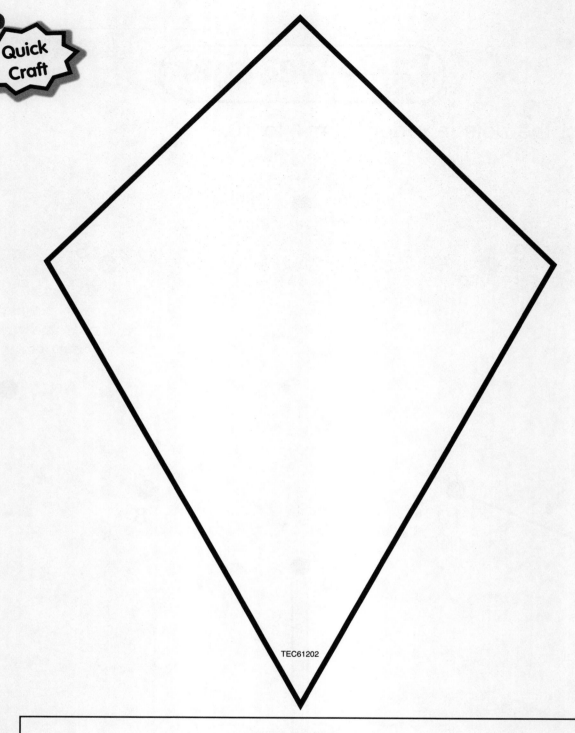

TEC61202

A Cool Kite

Materials: crepe paper, small cup of diluted glue, 1" tissue paper squares, paintbrush, scissors

Directions: Use the brush to cover the kite with glue. Then press tissue paper squares on the kite, overlapping the squares as desired. After the entire kite is covered, brush a thin layer of glue over the kite. When the glue is dry, cut on the bold line. Finally, attach a crepe paper tail.

Seriation Cards

Center: Make several copies of the largest umbrella card and an equal number of the largest raindrop card on page 119. Program each umbrella with a capital letter and each raindrop with a corresponding lowercase letter. A child matches each umbrella to its corresponding raindrop. **Matching uppercase and lowercase letters**

Seasonal Cards

Large group: Copy and cut out the spring seasonal cards on page 116 and discard the distracter cards. Use some of or all the seasonal cards to make a graph, similar to the one shown, on a piece of bulletin board paper. Help each child write her name on a sticky note. Assist each child in positioning the note in the column that represents what she likes about spring. After each child has placed her sticky note on the graph, ask questions about the number of students represented in each column, using words such as *more, fewer,* and *same.* **Graphing**

Bonus Activities

Finish the Picture

Spring

One day I found a <u>teddy bear</u> in a nest!

Individual: Program a copy of page 115 with the sentence shown and then copy the page to make a class supply. Give each child a copy of the programmed page. Ask him to complete the nest and then make a silly picture by drawing something that usually would not be inside a nest. Have each youngster write in the blank or dictate to you the name of the person or object he drew. Then invite each child to share his drawing. **Writing**

Math Mat and Manipulatives

Small group: Cut apart the ladybug cards from a copy of page 121 for each child in a small group. (Discard the number cards or save them for a different activity.) Program the back of the cards with shapes. Give each child a copy of page 120 and a set of ladybug cards. Help her place ten cards on her leaf, shape-side down. Then have her stack her five extra cards on the gray box. In turn, each child flips over a card on the leaf and identifies the shape. If she is correct, she "flies" her ladybug off the mat and sets it aside. If she is incorrect, she places the card at the bottom of the stack, takes a card from the top, and places it shape-side down on her mat. Play continues until a child has cleared all the cards off her mat. **Shape identification**

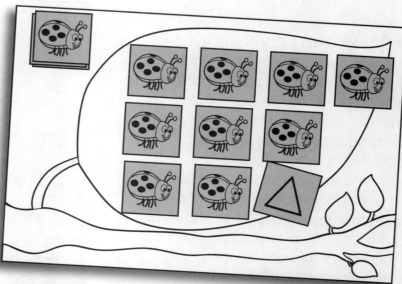

St. Patrick's Day

Note to the teacher: Have each child finish the picture by completing the shamrock. If desired, have her spread thinned glue tinted with green food coloring on the shamrock and then sprinkle green glitter on the glue. Post the pictures with the title "Shimmering Shamrocks."

Listen and Do

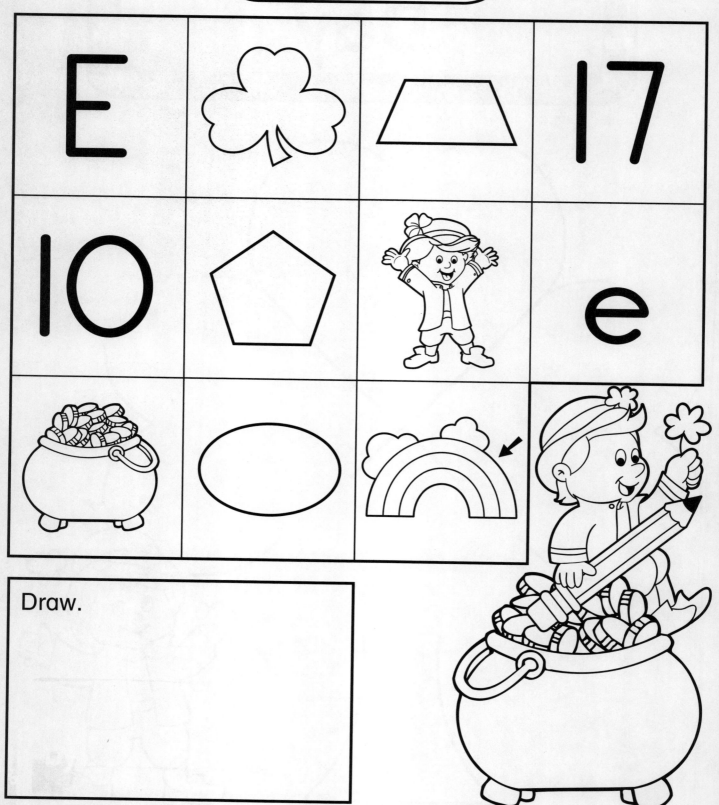

Draw.

Note to the teacher: Provide oral directions, such as "Circle the shamrock" or "Color the oval green," for each child to follow. Then specify what you would like her to draw in the empty box at the bottom of the page.

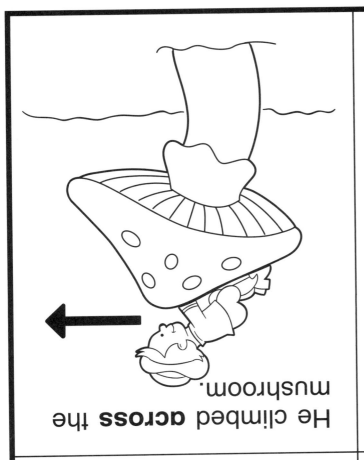

He climbed **across** the mushroom.

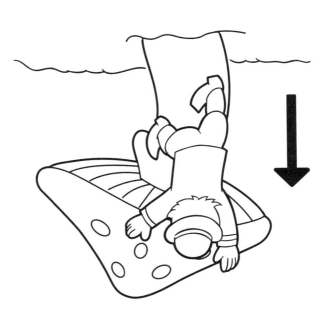

The leprechaun climbed **up** the mushroom.

He climbed **down** the mushroom.

Which Way Did He Go?

Name _____

Everything Seasonal & Holiday • ©The Mailbox® Books • TEC61202

Fold-and-Go Booklet: To make a booklet, cut on the bold line. Fold along the thin horizontal line (keeping the programming to the outside) and then fold along the thin vertical line (keeping the cover to the outside).

133

Quick Craft

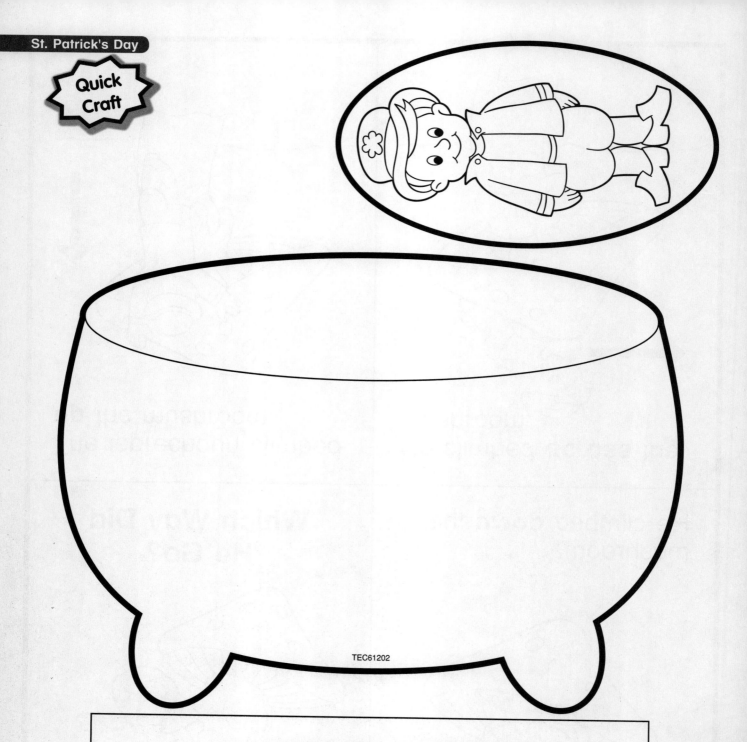

TEC61202

Leprechaun's Pot of Gold

Materials: 9" x 12" sheet of green construction paper, black construction paper scraps, gold glitter, markers, scissors, glue

Directions: Tear black paper scraps into small pieces and glue them to the pot. Cut out the pot and glue it to the green paper. Spread glue above the pot; then sprinkle gold glitter on the glue. Finally, color and cut out the leprechaun and glue him near his pot of gold.

Easter

Note to the teacher: Have each child finish the picture by completing the egg and decorating it as he wishes. If desired, cut out each egg and display it in a large basket cutout with the title "An 'Eggs-traordinary' Class!"

Listen and Do

Draw.

Note to the teacher: Provide oral directions, such as "Color the carrot orange" or "Circle the rectangle," for each child to follow. Then specify what you would like him to draw in the empty box at the bottom of the page.

Pretty Eggs

Color the matching
eggs in each row.

  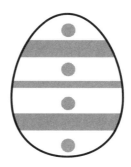 

  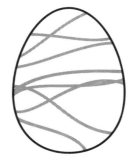 

Math Mat: Copy and cut out the carrot and number cards from page 139. Use the mat and the cards to provide a variety of hands-on math skill practice, including counting, number sets, comparing sets, number combinations, ordinal numbers, and odd and even numbers.

Everything Seasonal & Holiday • ©The Mailbox® Books • TEC61202

Carrot and Number Cards
Use with the math mat on page 138.

🥕 TEC61202	🥕 TEC61202	🥕 TEC61202	🥕 TEC61202	🥕 TEC61202
🥕 TEC61202	🥕 TEC61202	🥕 TEC61202	🥕 TEC61202	🥕 TEC61202
🥕 TEC61202	🥕 TEC61202	🥕 TEC61202	🥕 TEC61202	🥕 TEC61202
1 TEC61202	2 TEC61202	3 TEC61202	4 TEC61202	5 TEC61202
6 TEC61202	7 TEC61202	8 TEC61202	9 TEC61202	10 TEC61202
11 TEC61202	12 TEC61202	13 TEC61202	14 TEC61202	15 TEC61202

Name _____

Looking at Letters

✏️ Circle the matching letters in each row.

r	k	r	r	j	r

| w | c | c | c | t | c |

| b | m | b | b | v | b |

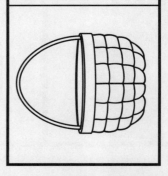

Easter Time!
My favorite thing to do on Easter is

by _____

Everything Seasonal & Holiday • ©The Mailbox® Books • TEC61202

Class Book Page: Have each child respond to the prompt orally (for you to write) or in writing. Then have him illustrate and personalize his work. Publish the pages in a class book titled "Easter Is 'Egg-citing'!"

141

Hunting for Eggs

Draw.
Help Chick find the basket.

Quick Craft

Baby Chick's Cozy Nest

Materials: 9" x 12" sheet of white construction paper, container of yellow paint, large craft feather (to paint with), small yellow craft feathers, orange construction paper triangle (beak), nest-making materials (such as light brown crinkle strips or pieces of light brown yarn), scissors, glue

Directions: Use the large craft feather to paint the chick. When the paint is dry, cut on the bold line. Glue the cutout to the center of the paper. Next, glue yellow craft feathers to the chick's body so they resemble wings; then glue the beak in place. Finally, glue nest-making materials around the bottom of the chick.

Finish the Picture

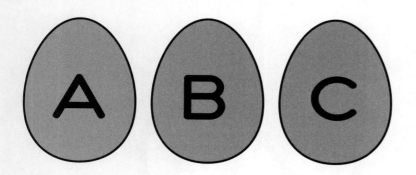

Large group: Complete the egg pattern on page 135; then cut out and program 26 construction paper copies of the egg, each with a different letter. Secretly hide the eggs in the classroom. Then send your students on an egg hunt. After all 26 eggs have been found, have students place them in order from *A* to *Z* using an alphabet strip as a guide. **Ordering letters**

Math Mat and Manipulatives

Partners: Give each child a copy of the math mat from page 138 along with a set of carrot and number cards from page 139, cut apart. Each student places his number cards facedown. To begin, each youngster takes a number card. Then he places the corresponding number of carrot cards on his mat. The students compare the sets of carrots to determine which set has more or fewer or whether the two sets are equal. Then each child removes the carrots from his mat and sets the number card aside. Play continues in this manner with the remaining number cards. **Comparing sets**

Earth Day

Everything Seasonal & Holiday • ©The Mailbox® Books • TEC61202

Note to the teacher: Have each child finish the picture by completing the recycling bin and drawing hair and facial details on the child. Help reinforce youngsters' understanding of different recyclable materials by having each child color the cereal box brown, the plastic milk container yellow, and the can of corn green.

Name _____

Listen and Do

Z	(tree)	(star)	9
(earth)	(diamond)	(lightbulb)	z
2	(sink)	(truck)	(flower)

Draw.

Note to the teacher: Provide oral directions, such as "Cross off the lowercase *z*" or "Color the lightbulb yellow," for each child to follow. Then specify what you would like her to draw in the empty box at the bottom of the page.

Helping the Earth

I can help the earth by

by _____

Class Book Page: Have each child respond to the prompt orally (for you to write) or in writing. Then have her illustrate and personalize her work. Publish the pages in a class book titled "Our Precious Earth."

147

Quick Craft

Help Protect
Our
Planet Earth!

TEC61202

Our Wonderful World

Materials: sheet of black construction paper, blue and green powdered tempera paints, spray bottle filled with water, scissors, glue

Directions: Lightly sprinkle both paints on the earth pattern; then spray a fine mist of water on the paint. After the paint is dry, cut on the bold line; then glue the cutout to the center of the construction paper. If desired, add foil stars to the paper around the cutout.

Cinco de Mayo

Note to the teacher: Have each child finish the picture by completing the maracas and decorating them as desired. Post the pictures with the title "Celebrate Cinco de Mayo!"

Listen and Do

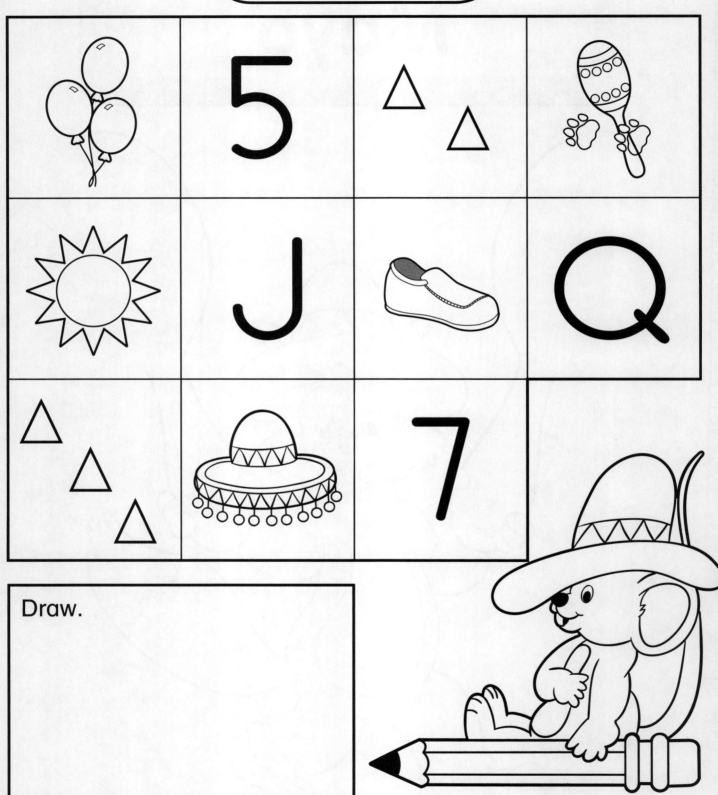

Draw.

Note to the teacher: Provide oral directions, such as "Circle the letter *Q*" or "Color the box that shows three triangles," for each child to follow. Then specify what you would like him to draw in the empty box at the bottom of the page.

Bird hits the **middle** of the piñata.

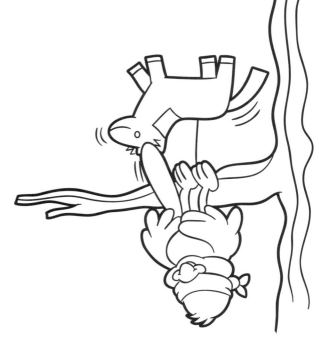

Bird hits the **top** of the piñata.

Bird hits the **bottom** of the piñata.

Bird Hits the Piñata!

Name _____

Everything Seasonal & Holiday • ©The Mailbox® Books • TEC61202

Fold-and-Go Booklet: To make a booklet, cut on the bold line. Fold along the thin horizontal line (keeping the programming to the outside) and then fold along the thin vertical line (keeping the cover to the outside).

151

A Super Sombrero

Connect the dots in order from 1 to 15.

Mother's Day

MOM   MOM   MOM   MOM   MOM

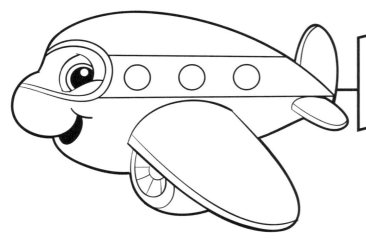

I Love you, Mom!

Note to the teacher: Have each child finish the picture by drawing a picture of herself with her mother on the bottom half of the page. Post the pictures with the title "Moms Are Magnificent!"

Listen and Do

Draw.

Note to the teacher: Provide oral directions, such as "Color the butterfly blue" or "Circle the umbrella," for each child to follow. Then specify what you would like her to draw in the empty box at the bottom of the page.

Moms Are Special

I love my mom because

by _____

Everything Seasonal & Holiday • ©The Mailbox® Books • TEC61202

Class Book Page: Have each child respond to the prompt orally (for you to write) or in writing. Then have her illustrate and personalize her work. Publish the pages in a class book titled "Marvelous Moms!"

Quick Craft

Happy Mother's Day!

TEC61202

Flowers For Mom

Materials: 9" x 12" sheet of construction paper folded in half (card), colorful tissue paper squares, markers, scissors, glue

Directions: Decorate the vase as desired; then cut it out and glue it near the bottom of the front of the card. Draw green stems and leaves above the vase. Crumple tissue paper squares to make flowers and glue one to the top of each stem. When the glue is dry, illustrate and personalize the inside of the card.

Summer

Note to the teacher: Have each child finish the picture by adding facial details and hair so the child resembles himself. Then have him draw in the background something he plans to do over the summer. Stack the completed pages and bind them into a class book titled "Our Summer Plans."

Name_____

Listen and Do

Draw.

Note to the teacher: Provide oral directions, such as "Circle the strawberry" or "Color the sun yellow," for each child to follow. Then specify what you would like him to draw in the empty box at the bottom of the page.

Matching Castles

Color the matching sand castles in each row.

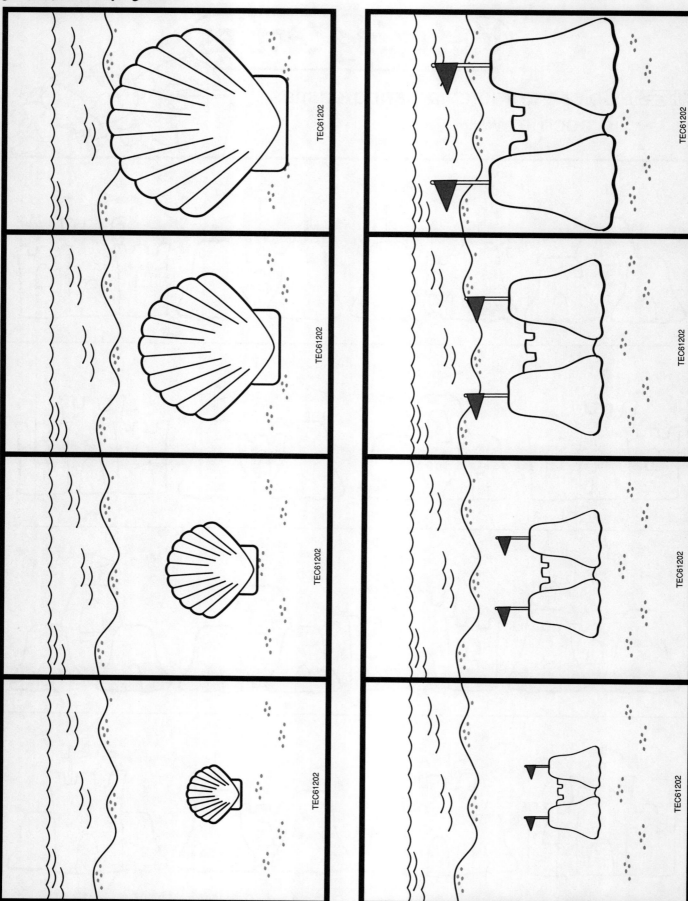

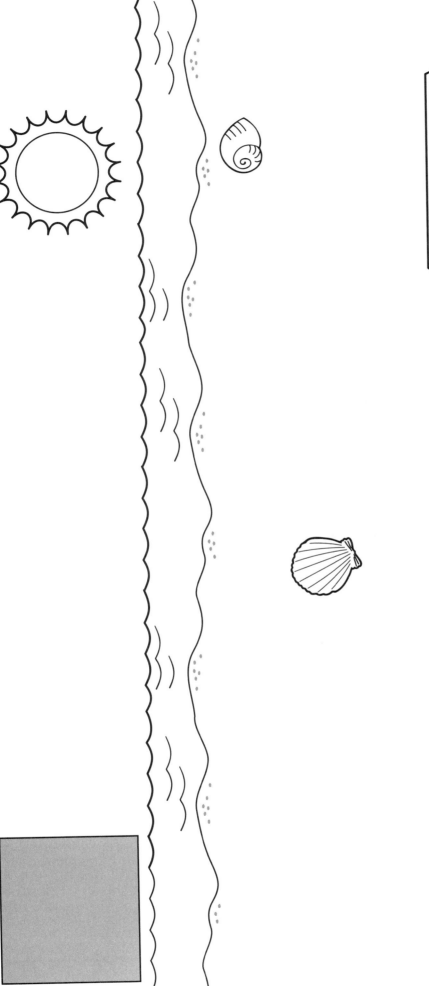

Welcome to
Crab Beach

Everything Seasonal & Holiday • ©The Mailbox® Books • TEC61202

Math Mat: Copy and cut out the crab and number cards from page 162. Use the mat and cards to provide a variety of hands-on math skill practice, including counting, number sets, comparing sets, number combinations, ordinal numbers, and odd and even numbers.

Crab and Number Cards
Use with the math mat on page 161.

TEC61202	TEC61202	TEC61202	TEC61202	TEC61202
TEC61202	TEC61202	TEC61202	TEC61202	TEC61202
TEC61202	TEC61202	TEC61202	TEC61202	TEC61202
1 TEC61202	**2** TEC61202	**3** TEC61202	**4** TEC61202	**5** TEC61202
6 TEC61202	**7** TEC61202	**8** TEC61202	**9** TEC61202	**10** TEC61202
11 TEC61202	**12** TEC61202	**13** TEC61202	**14** TEC61202	**15** TEC61202

S Is for Sun

✂ Cut.

🗴 Glue the pictures that begin like ☀.

Name _____

Looking at Letters

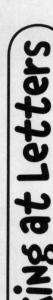 Circle the matching letters in each row.

	r	w	w	w	h	w
	b	b	b	t	k	b
	c	s	s	s	m	s

Everything Seasonal & Holiday • ©The Mailbox® Books • TEC61202

bell.

rhymes with

Shell

bun.

rhymes with

Sun

 Cone

rhymes with

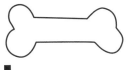 bone.

 Summer Rhymes

Name _____

Fold-and-Go Booklet: To make a booklet, cut on the bold line. Fold along the thin horizontal line (keeping the programming to the outside) and then fold along the thin vertical line (keeping the cover to the outside).

Name _____

Sunny Rays

✂ Cut.

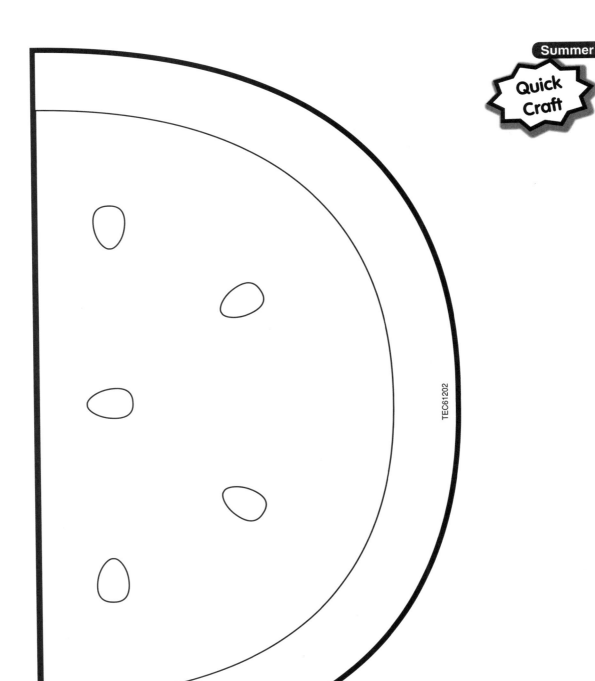

Quick Craft

TEC61202

A Sweet Slice

Materials: gelatin paint (sugar-free watermelon gelatin mixed with a small amount of water), paintbrush, black and green crayons, scissors

Directions: Color the watermelon rind green and the seeds black. Then paint the watermelon slice with the gelatin paint. When the watermelon slice is dry, cut it out.

Seriation Cards

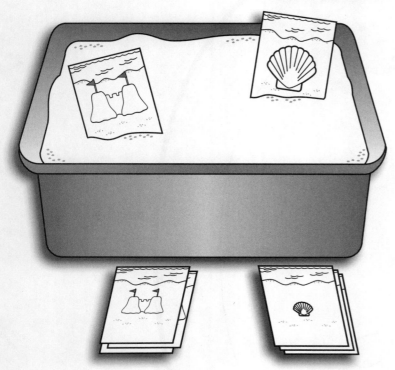

Center: Laminate several copies of the cards on page 160 and cut them apart. Hide the cards in a large container of sand. A child finds each card and places it in one of two piles: seashells or sand castles. Then she sorts each pile of cards by size. **Sorting**

Quick Craft

Center: Make a few copies of the watermelon slice from page 167 on red construction paper. Cut out the slices and laminate them for durability. Then hole-punch each slice along the outer edge. Tie one end of a length of green yarn to the hole at one end of the slice. Wrap the other end of the yarn with masking tape for easy lacing. A youngster threads the yarn through the holes in a slice to make a rind. **Fine-motor skills**

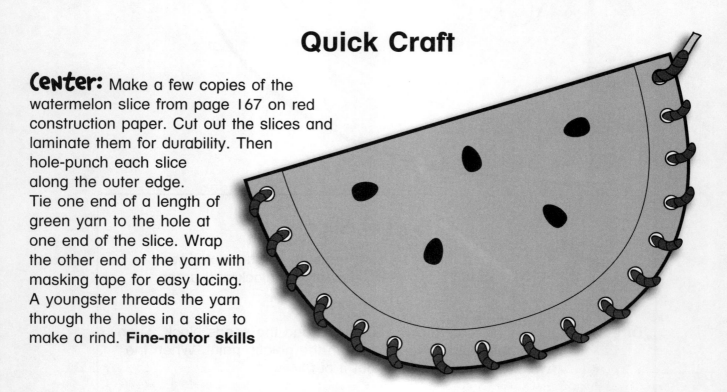

Father's Day

DAD DAD DAD DAD DAD

You brighten my day, Dad!

Note to the teacher: Have each child finish the picture by drawing a picture of herself with her father on the bottom half of the page. Stack the completed pages and bind them into a class book titled "Fathers Are Fabulous!"

Name_____

Listen and Do

Draw.

Note to the teacher: Provide oral directions, such as "Circle the picture that begins with the /t/ sound" or "Color the car red," for each child to follow. Then specify what you would like her to draw in the empty box at the bottom of the page.

Dad starts like **doughnut.**

Dad starts like **dog.**

Dad starts like **doll.**

Dad Starts Like...

Name _____

Fold-and-Go Booklet: To make a booklet, cut on the bold line. Fold along the thin horizontal line (keeping the programming to the outside) and then fold along the thin vertical line (keeping the cover to the outside).

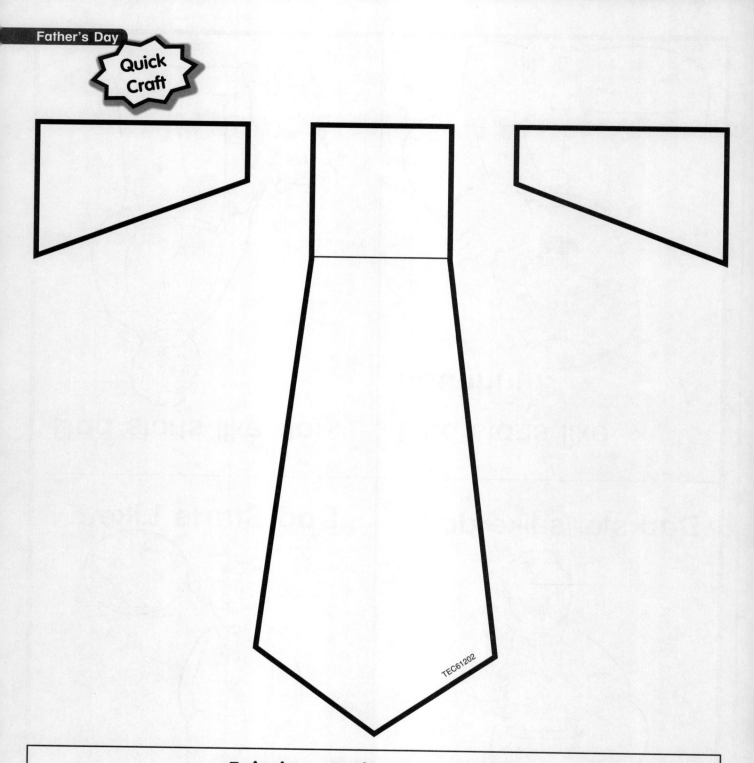

Quick Craft

Fabulous Father's Day Card

Materials: 9" x 12" sheet of construction paper folded in half, colorful tissue paper scraps, scissors, glue, paintbrush, diluted glue

Directions: Tear tissue paper scraps into small pieces and glue them to the tie; then brush a thin coat of diluted glue over the tissue paper. After the glue dries, cut on the bold line, trimming off any excess tissue paper. Cut out the collar pieces. Glue the tie and the collar pieces to the top edge of the folded paper. Finally, sign your name inside the card.

Fourth of July

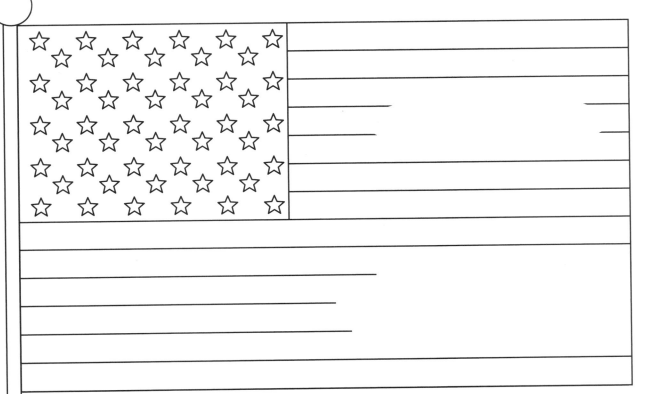

Note to the teacher: Have each child finish the picture by completing the flag. Then have him color the flag. Post the pictures with the title "A Star-Spangled Fourth of July!"

173

Listen and Do

Draw.

Everything Seasonal & Holiday • ©The Mailbox® Books • TEC61202

Note to the teacher: Provide oral directions, such as "Circle the picnic basket" or "Color the box that has more than one star," for each child to follow. Then specify what you would like him to draw in the empty box at the bottom of the page.

Bear sees **four** fireworks.

Bear sees **two** fireworks.

Bear sees **zero** fireworks.

How Many Fireworks Does Bear See?

Name _____

Everything Seasonal & Holiday • ©The Mailbox® Books • TEC61202

Fold-and-Go Booklet: To make a booklet, cut on the bold line. Fold along the thin horizontal line (keeping the programming to the outside) and then fold along the thin vertical line (keeping the cover to the outside).

175

Time to Celebrate!

Draw.
Help Skunk find Rabbit.